Lean Healthcare

By Ade Asefeso MCIPS MBA

Second Edition

ISBN-13: 978-1499542301

ISBN-10: 1499542305

Publisher: AA Global Sourcing Ltd
Website: http://www.aaglobalsourcing.com

Table of Contents

Disclaimer

This publication is designed to provide competent and reliable information regarding the subject matter covered. However, it is sold with the understanding that the author and publisher are not engaged in rendering professional advice. The authors and publishers specifically disclaim any liability that is incurred from the use or application of contents of this book.

If you purchased this book without a cover you should be aware that this book may have been stolen property and reported as "unsold and destroyed" to the publisher. In this case neither the author nor the publisher has received any payment for this "stripped book."

Dedication

This book is dedicated to the hundreds of thousands of incredible souls in the world who have weathered through the up and down of recent recession.

To my family and friends who seems to have been sent here to teach me something about who I am supposed to be. They have nurtured me, challenged me, and even opposed me…. But at every juncture has taught me!

This book is dedicated to my lovely boys, Thomas, Michael and Karl. Teaching them to manage their finance will give them the lives they deserve. They have taught me more about life, presence, and energy management than anything I have done in my life.

Chapter 1: Introduction

What exactly is Lean?

There are a variety of techniques and tools available to achieve the objectives associated with Lean Thinking. Lean, however, is not simply a set of tools. Lean is a problem solving approach for continuous daily improvement. Lean is about creating increased value for your customers (patients) by eliminating wasteful activities. Any activity or process that consumes resources or adds cost or time without creating value is a target for elimination.

One of the important aspects of Lean is the focus on "service-level" improvements. Think in terms of value-stream improvements (e.g., outpatient surgery or inpatient obstetrical care value streams).

Improvements made along an entire value stream or service will result in increased efficiency, improved quality, and increased safety with dramatic cost savings.

The following are key points of Lean Thinking that you must not lose sight of if you are going to be successful in its application:
- Each employee will arrive at work every day thinking about how they are going to improve their work environment; with this commitment, there is continuous daily improvement.

- Measurement is essential. Understanding the value stream baseline and the subsequent improvement achieved is critical.
- Measurement is key to continuous improvement and provides a basis for understanding your accomplishments.

UK and American healthcare are in crisis. The industry is struggling with skyrocketing costs, poor quality, nursing shortages and employee dissatisfaction; all symptoms of deeper problems inherent in the system itself.

More and more healthcare providers are realizing the imperative of improving quality and safety and eliminating waste as strategies for responding to the challenges. Enter Lean Healthcare, the "how to" of managing change and creating continuous improvement.

Lean Healthcare is not just another project: it's a way to transform your entire organization into a safe and high-quality, high-performing healthcare delivery system.

Lean Healthcare can eliminate many obstacles to excellence, such as cumbersome information technology systems, worker frustration, and inadvertent errors and oversights that can increase patient safety risks. Surprisingly few improvements require costly or sweeping high-tech fixes. Most often, simple, well designed interactions based on scientific observations and experiments bring nearly unimaginable improvement, fast.

In 2010, shortly after I left corporate world I had lunch with a doctor from one of the UK's regional larger hospitals. He had recently seen a Toyota-based "lean" approach dramatically reduce infection rates in his hospital but predicted that it would never really take hold as a movement in healthcare. It could work in isolated areas where it was championed by strong individuals, he argued, but it was too much of a culture change for the industry as a whole to embrace.

At the time, I didn't know if he was right. The field of Lean Healthcare was very young in the UK then. There were only two books and a handful of articles available on the topic. I could count on one hand the number of conferences or training programs that touched on the subject. Working for twenty years in lean manufacturing environment, I had seen the Toyota/Lean approach improve profit, reduce cost, increase staff satisfaction, and improve quality and safety. But the ability of doctors and hospital administrators to grasp its full potential on an organization or industry-wide basis was still up in the air.

That same year, in 2010, I was recruited to lead a lean transformation at a local hospital in the UK, and in the last three years the field of Lean Healthcare has exploded.

This year, as hospitals wonder not whether they will lose revenue with the coming reform, but how much they will lose, the Toyota Production System is having its day in healthcare. Evolved from the rubble of post-war Japan, there was no room for waste of any kind at Toyota, so the company developed just-in-time production, tightly standardized work to achieve reliable outcomes, and invested heavily in training a workforce that would continuously ferret out and eliminate waste wherever it sprouted.

Looking ahead, the way to meet the demands of an increasingly exacting payer community and the needs of patients with high service expectations is not to cut costs across the board, but to follow a Toyota-style path of identifying and reducing any activity that does not provide a direct service to your customer or patient.

After the dramatic turnaround of the Emergency Department of our local hospital, in which we used Toyota/Lean methods to redesign patient flow (bringing our overall patient satisfaction from the 61% 90% in a single year), we turned to dozens of other improvement efforts all over the hospital. Some have been high level affecting the entire hospital like creating a dedicated Observation Unit for patients awaiting diagnosis. Others have been as simple as reducing the number of times a nurse has to leave a patient's room by providing pill crushers for every room. Most exciting, however, is that having trained over 50% of the workforce (1,000+ employees) over the last three years in the basics of Toyota/Lean thinking, the hospital have seen more and more improvements cropping up in every department. Some originate with leaders, but many come from frontline staff.

In impatience department we may look for the quick fix; the one big change that will give the hospital back millions of pounds in cost, or an hour a day in lost time for the staff. But Toyota races like the tortoise. Those huge strokes of waste cutting are rare, and most organizations have found them by now. What is left are the hundreds of small annoyances that riddle our complex healthcare delivery systems. The little errors and inefficiencies in our days that drain away the capacity to serve patients a few seconds or minutes at a time; the missing medication, the ambiguous job instructions, the ineligible chart, the incomplete shift report, the complicated phone tree. To plug those hundreds of drainage holes takes a disciplined organizational culture of relentless and continuous improvement with all hands on deck. One administrator or manager couldn't possibly find all those holes, let alone know how to plug them effectively. Every employee's critical eyes and creativity need to be harnessed in reducing waste.

When I look ahead, this is what I see. Armies of caregivers and support staff, equipped with disciplined ways of understanding and improving their work, and supported by a leadership who understand that Lean Healthcare is not a program, but a culture. A culture ideally suited for our time.

Chapter 2: Healthcare Sector Requires Clients Satisfaction

The Healthcare profession is facing growing challenges of:

1. Cost of materials.
2. Staff shortages.
3. Increased demand.
4. Increased stress on their staff.
5. Greater potential for mistakes.
6. Increased dissatisfaction from patients/clients because of long wait times and poor service.
7. Financial restraints from insurance companies and governments.
8. Increased media attention and distractions.

Traditionally these problems have been solved by providing more staff, more money, more space or a combination of all these factors. Sometimes the answer is simply that the patient must wait longer for treatment.

The Healthcare sector requires the ultimate in client/patient satisfaction purely by the nature of the service it provides. A growing number of healthcare organizations are applying the Lean principles to increase their effectiveness.

The Lean approach focuses on two major objectives: Customer satisfaction and flow whilst simultaneously improving staff satisfaction and safety.

When the transformation is completed properly it affects the organization's end-to-end processes, plus the culture. The positive and usually immediate impacts include the speed, cost and quality of service. Once lean implementation is underway, the entire staff (doctors, nurses, technicians, and support staff) and the patients all 'see' and 'feel' the impact. There is a huge shift in culture and thinking and everyone starts to work as a team and as part of the Value Stream not in department or silos. The stresses are removed and staff are able to focus on applying their skills instead of spending time on the non-value activities.

The principles of Lean can be applied to a range of healthcare environments, such as hospitals, family practice units, laboratories, residential homes and medical supply facilities large and small. Amazing results have been achieved in just a few weeks by eliminating wasteful activities that over time have become part of the everyday system/processes, freeing up time for staff to do real value added work. These improvements are beneficial to everyone; patients, doctors, nurses and administrators.

Healthcare is the perfect environment to implement Lean and streamline complex processes.

The staff are motivated and are passionate about giving the best care to their patients/clients. All they need is the relevant knowledge and methods to transform their processes and thinking to meet the challenges they are facing both today and in the future.

Healthcare staff are doing an amazing job considering the processes they have to work with are less than perfect. The processes are the problem and need to be fixed so that our healthcare workers can do their jobs efficiently.

There is an abundance of empirical and anecdotal evidence to support the use of lean principles in modern healthcare. However eager employees returning from Lean training enthused and excited about the prospect of introducing lean into their organization may have their hopes extinguished by a healthy dose of reality when they return to their offices.

The case for lean is undeniable. The economics of modern healthcare demand value added processes, fluid patient movement through clinical interventions, and the perpetual absence of waste.

Lean is ideally suited to address that challenge, but the transformation of an organization into a lean environment does consume resources time, space, effort, and of course, money.

Lean practitioners, especially those champions introducing lean principles to an organization for the first time, need to acknowledge that lean is, in fact, an investment. In the face of budget constraints, funding shortages, overworked management teams and many competing priorities, we need practical tools for demonstrating a quantifiable return on lean investments.

Executives make resource allocation decisions based on such criteria as patient care impact, alignment with strategic directions, and the relative size of a project's return on investment (ROI). Lean practitioners and Kaizen facilitators need to become proficient at calculating the financial impact of lean endeavours.

It is useful, therefore, to have measurable outputs for lean initiatives and quantifiable results that illustrate their return.

Dealing with limited resources is certainly not new to Hospital administrators, but the application of lean principles may provide new ways to address the challenges it creates. Time, for example, is a limited resource traditionally sourced by new hires or additional budgeted hours. In a lean world, time is created by eliminating non-value-added activities from key processes.

As waste is identified and eliminated, time capacity is created and staff can be redeployed into value-added activities. Similarly, physical space capacity issues have traditionally been addressed through renovations, additions, or redevelopment.

Lean provides for workplace redesign strategies (5S, FIFO lanes, Kanbans, etc.) that typically reduce physical space requirements. Reclaimed space can be reassigned to avoid future capital costs and can accommodate value-added patient care or revenue generating activities.

Money, of course, is commonly understood to be in short supply, and lean efforts that lead to cost reductions or cost avoidances contribute directly to the budgetary challenges facing all hospitals.

Calculating the full return on a Kaizen event can be challenging, but enormously important in terms of demonstrating the power of lean. The real contribution of events that create time, space or financial capacity is tied to the value created through the redeployment of freed up resources. That new value might be cost avoidance (e.g. when people are redeployed to add value in other processes rather than outsourcing or recruiting), or it might lead to new or increased revenue streams. For example, if an initiative to improve on-time discharges leads to an increase in billable room differentials (upgrades from semi-private to private), then this new revenue is a direct return on the investment in the event.

Whatever the outcome of a lean initiative or a Kaizen event, the team involved must be tasked with identifying cause/effect relationships and the positive consequences of any change. Often, one cost avoidance might lead to a pure savings in another area, or might open up revenue streams never before available.

Practitioners who are skilled at quantifying, in financial terms, the full and future impact of lean transformations will have an easier time advocating for future investments in lean.

Chapter 3: Why Lean Principles Are Ideal for Healthcare

Paediatricians and other healthcare professionals can better serve patients through Lean. Lean management has recently been implemented by numerous hospitals and other healthcare providers.

It seems everyday a new story showcases outstanding results from a Lean transition in a hospital or clinical setting.

For instance, a Canadian hospital cut the time it took for heart attack patients to receive angioplasty from 90 minutes to 37, just by learning from Lean that it was unnecessary to have two separate, similarly qualified doctors make the same diagnosis.

Why does Lean work so well for health care?

Health Care and Manufacturing Commonalities

The automotive manufacturing industry, where Lean originated, is based on a large group of competent professionals, each doing a small and highly specialized task to ultimately produce an incredibly complex final product.

Likewise, healthcare consists of a diverse array of highly competent specialists, each fully aware of his or her duties and well trained in performing them, but potentially less aware or even mistrustful of others in the process.

Individual Empowerment Works

Lean manufacturing brings manufacturing floor workers together by empowering each individual to find efficiencies and opportunities for continuous improvement in his or her area of responsibility. Workers are called upon to step to the plate and say, "I can do this better and I can tell you how."

In healthcare, the same tactic works; every nurse, doctor, phlebotomist, and doctor's assistant likely feels in some way constrained by managerial policies that prevent him or her from performing at the highest levels.

For instance, in the US a doctor felt constrained and de-motivated by policies that forced them to wait for a cardiologist to confirm their diagnoses before helping heart attack patients. When the doctor and cardiologists were tasked with creating a methodology permitting a more rapid procession (or, product flow?) from intake to angioplasty, the cardiologists decided they were comfortable with the doctors diagnosing heart attacks, provided a uniform diagnostic procedure was followed.

As a friend of mine says: "(Lean) leads to much more staff engagement. When they are put on the pedestal as "You are who matters when it comes to delivering better value to the patient that is a refreshing change."

Focus on Results

In the automotive industry, American manufacturers fell behind Toyota for decades because they remained committed to products and processes that were not working. Transitioning to a Lean, results-oriented process that demands results and continuous improvement of key performance indicators resurrected the United States auto industry.

In healthcare, there is no way to say "We are making a great product that just hasn't caught on full speed ahead!" If patient outcomes are poor, the delivery of care is poor. Lean recognizes this and forces results-orientation, focused on patient outcomes. Individual theories about healthcare delivery can be tested, but if they don't support continuous improvement, they must go no matter whose ego is at stake.

Chapter 4: Lean Methodology in Healthcare Improvement

Lean is a type of quality improvement methodology which has been implemented in many industries. Its principles and practices also have been applied to healthcare organizations with success. This has been accomplished with refinement for the nuances of health care. Lean is a process management philosophy which has its roots in manufacturing and technology.

Significance: Value

A significant component of Lean is the concept of value; the theoretical concept of value, the measurement of value, and the tangible processes behind delivering value. Lean is unique in that it accounts for the reduction of waste in order to achieve both real and potential value. Recovering this value can present itself in the form of saved costs or other tangibles. Lean thinking dictates that the expenditure of resources for any purpose other than delivering value to the customer is considered to be wasteful. The reduced expenditure of time, money, and resources is thought to bring additional bottom-line benefit to the customer. The customer-centric focus of Lean thinking is especially relevant to health care. Broader levels of patient/customer satisfaction are constantly being sought. This mode of thinking has been brought on by increased competition among organizations and the need to differentiate services.

It is recognized that providing complete customer satisfaction can be vastly beneficial to health care organizations. Customer satisfaction can be an equally important measure of an organization's performance as the delivery of quality health outcomes. Lean thinking dictates that processes and methods must be efficiently optimized with the needs of customers in mind in order for organizations to be fully effective.

Problem Addressed: Waste

Lean focuses on the maximization of process velocity through the reduction of waste. It provides tools for analyzing process flow and delay times at each activity in a process. The focal point is the separation of "value-added" from "non-value-added" work. This is complemented by tools which aide in the identification and elimination of root causes of non-valued activities. The primary problem addressed by Lean is waste, which can affect value in a number of ways. It may result in lower quality products, higher costs, less favourable customer experiences, excessive time or effort expended to complete goals, or fewer resources available for innovation which could provide potential value at a future date. Waste can be found in people, processes, tangibles, and other areas. Eliminating waste through the lens of Lean production can help to achieve the goals of healthcare organizations. There are eight generally identifiable centres of waste; overproduction, waiting (time on hand), unnecessary transport or conveyance, over-processing or incorrect processing, excess inventory,

24

unnecessary human movement, defects, and unused employee creativity.

Process: Root Cause Analysis

A crucial process in Lean is the identification of waste through root cause analysis. Root cause analysis in Lean involves a method called 5-Whys. This method rapidly identifies root causes and aides in determining the relationship between multiple root causes. It can be learned quickly and does not require statistical analysis. This method is especially effective for an implementation team in the initial stages of problem exploration. The application of this strategy involves asking a series of why-related questions to drill down into a problem area. Asking progressive questions about a perceived difficulty forces team members to think critically about the actual sources of waste and inefficiency. It is suggested that at least five questions (5-Whys) are posed to arrive at the root cause, though a root cause may be discovered in more or less inquires.

The following is an example of a 5-Whys exercise used in a hypothetical hospital setting:

(Q1) Why are patients being diverted to neighbouring hospitals?
(A1) Because wait times for our hospital are exceeding industry norms.

(Q2) Why are our wait times exceeding industry norms?
(A2) Because patient volume is exceeding capacity.

(Q3) Why is patient volume exceeding capacity?
(A3) Because not enough hospital beds are available.

(Q4) Why are not enough hospital beds available?
(A4) Because hospital patients are not being discharged efficiently.

(Q5) Why are hospital patients not being discharged efficiently?
(A5) Because ER (Emergency Room) staff is not following best practices for proper discharge.

In this example, waste in the throughput process comes from incorrect processing. Once hospital management determines the root cause they can implement further training, ensure compliance with existing standards, or eliminate other barriers. In this case the hospital might consider implementing a training program to ensure that ER staff is following best practices for patient discharge. The hospital might also conduct additional 5-Whys analyses to uncover other problem areas. Once root causes of waste are uncovered, the elimination of waste or other related action plans can be executed.

Sources of waste

Sources of waste vary greatly by industry. The majority of waste encountered by healthcare organizations occurs in flow and throughput. As a result, Lean implementations in this field are primarily focused on the elimination of waste in staffing and staff/patient processes. Unlike manufacturing industries most healthcare organizations have very little inventory. Thus, some of the Lean concepts related to inventory control are less applicable to healthcare. Healthcare organizations typically spend a larger percentage of operating expenses on overhead and labour costs. This can account for 50 percent of the operating costs while inventory is in the range of 2 percent.

Understanding waste in throughput entails a comprehension of the relationships between process variables and costs. Costs are not causes of waste but are indicators of interrelationships between processes. While the ultimate goal of most Lean implementations is to recover costs as tangible benefits, eliminating costs without fully understanding processes is problematic. Looking at the types of cost recovery is essential to determining an action plan.

Solution: Cost Recovery

The ultimate goal of most Lean implementations is to attain a tangible benefit, often in the form of a cost recovery. However, not all process improvement opportunities will result in immediate returns. The actual realization of a benefit depends on the nature of the improvement as well as the additional steps that management takes to achieve it.

There are three types of cost recovery through the elimination of waste: Type 1, Type 2, and Type 3.

In a Type 1 situation the process throughput improvement will yield a direct cost recovery. For example, a process improvement that reduces length of patient stay would recover costs in the form of reduced resources expended.

In a Type 2 situation, the process improvement saves time but does not result in cost recovery without additional hours worked per unit of service. A provider may spend less time per patient because of reduced length of stay but scheduling will need to be adjusted in order to capitalize on the benefit to workflow.

Lastly, Type 3 yields savings in the form of immediate optimization of capacity. In this situation a process improvement in an emergency room, for example, may allow a provider to see more patients in the same staffed time without additional action taken by management. This is similar to a Type 2 recovery but with no changes to scheduling. This can occur if the provider is willing to see more patients per unit of time and sufficient patient volume exists to achieve capacity. Maximum velocity is achieved without additional action needed to be carried out by management. These examples show that throughput improvement may not achieve an immediate benefit without other factors. It also brings to light the fact that throughput improvement may yield different benefits such as recovered costs; time saved, or increased revenues. Regardless of the actual benefit achieved and the way that it is realized, the ultimate outcome must increase bottom-line value and satisfaction to customers in some way.

Lean is a multifaceted approach to quality improvement which has tangible benefits to healthcare organizations. There are aspects which focus on reducing non value-added work and waste to achieve value in various ways. Successfully implementing Lean in healthcare depends on the setting involved and the motivation of management and teams. Healthcare encompasses a wide range of organizations and each has unique characteristics which must be considered in light of Lean processes.

Important considerations in implementing lean in any environment can be reduced to a few key points;

- Understanding the concept of value.
- Understanding waste and its sources.
- Learning how to determine and analyze root causes.
- Prioritizing multiple root causes.
- Devising methods to eliminate waste.
- Determining ways to recover costs or achieve benefits.
- Analyzing effectiveness and repeating steps if necessary.

In addition, it is important to note that eliminating waste through a Lean process may not immediately result in tangible benefit. Management must thoroughly analyze action plans and make adjustments based on actual outcomes. Additional steps may need to be taken following initial process improvements. This is especially relevant in healthcare where process throughput improvement and staffing are areas which are commonly targeted. These areas may involve more challenges when trying to extract benefit. Freeing time for providers cannot always be capitalized upon without other capacity and throughput improvements.

Scheduling or work flow functions may need to be overhauled in order for providers to increase overall process velocity and maximize value per unit for time. It is also crucial to realize that humans are not machines. Theoretical methods of quality improvement in Lean may not always be feasible to achieve at maximum levels. The Lean methodology developed by Toyota is very cognizant of respect for people. It is reflective of a collective culture and a holistic concept rather than a series of parts or steps. This is a fact which cannot be overlooked by management and teams when planning an implementation. People perform processes with normal human variation and improvements must be sensitive, appropriate, and sustainable.

Chapter 5: Information Technology's Role in the Lean Healthcare

The days of waiting for the users in clinical and operational areas to define their requirements and tell IT what to do are long gone.

I cut my teeth in Information Technology in the mid 1980's, not trying to give away my age!. It was referred to as Electronic Data Processing or EDP then. We prided ourselves in being systems oriented, uncommonly smart, thorough thinkers able to grasp technology and wield it on behalf of the organization. These were the days of computers as big as city blocks running high volume transactions (millions!) at 90% reliability with sub-second response time; a performance standard that is laughable today. It was the role of EDP to automate the business to increase capacity and standardize quality. Technical staff were routinely located in remote areas of the building; it was generally accepted that we could function just as well and maybe even better in isolation. Basements or converted out buildings with few windows and no connection to our users would suffice.

Social skills were a minimal job requirement. If we had one or two people who could navigate communications with the rest of the company that was fine. The career path of an EDP professional followed the implementation of technology from one business sector to another; manufacturing to service to finance to healthcare...okay, maybe not to healthcare! No need to understand the business or the customer to do our jobs. The total value of our work was in automating business processes so that companies could do more, faster. Our primary business was 'technology'. It was the role of the user to define requirements; we built exactly what they asked for, no more, no less. If they didn't get it right the first time, well, rework was expected. That is how it was and we liked it just fine.

Of course, not everyone felt as warm and fuzzy about this scenario as the folks in EDP. CEOs and CFOs felt hi-jacked too much money, too much mystery, no way to guarantee return on investment (ROI). Every project of any significance was at least 8 months long and 900 hours in the making. Bringing up new systems was a multiyear project with a guaranteed 'break in period that could wreak havoc on the business. If you were lucky; and luck was really the deciding factor, you could retain your customer base through the transition.

Enter the Personal Computer (PC), the mobile phone and the internet. Electronic Data Processing became Information Technology (IT). Next thing you knew everyone was sharing ideas, hiring expert consultants from the outside, buying software and running their own reports.

The gig was up. Users could now understand what IT did at least to some degree and to demand that IT learn the language and the value proposition of the business and make a positive difference.

Somehow this whole technological revolution missed the healthcare industry. Sure, we saw some innovation in high profile/high pounds areas like pharmacy and robotics but not at the bedside or clinical care setting. It just wasn't sexy enough. Inefficient paper based systems, memory based care delivery, rising costs and increasingly poor quality were hallmarks of healthcare then and remain in place today.

Healthcare has some serious catching up to do. People, process and technology issues must all be considered. The historical limitations of data access and use in healthcare settings have conditioned us to ask the same limited set of questions over and over. Today's tools and technology offer greatly expanded options to work with data. The challenge is to inform leaders of what is possible so that they can begin to leverage data to understand and then redesign care delivery processes for higher value.

Don't be confused; this is not a problem looking for a technology solution, no matter what the vendors say. There is a logical sequence to this effort that influences its success: first mindset, then skill-set and then tool-set.

Lean processes, the well-executed, data driven problem identification and solving processes used to deliver consistently higher quality, lower cost products in manufacturing and service industries are slowly making their way into healthcare with similarly spectacular results. The speed and impact of the lean journey for a healthcare system is dependent upon its ability to deliver a reliable flow of meaningful information across the enterprise to support continuous process improvement. In fact, comparative performance reporting is essential to the value improvement of a healthcare organization and the transformation of the larger healthcare system. Scientific thinking fed by timely and reliable data must signal best practice and motivate change in provider behaviours.

A lean culture engages the entire organization in identifying waste and redesigning work flows to deliver value to their customer. Lean is not a spectator sport and IT is no exception. The analytical staff must work side by side with their clinical and operational peers to understand and solve business problems. Capacity issues are being felt across the healthcare.

Chapter 6: Eight Waste in Healthcare

There is a tremendous amount of waste occurring in the healthcare industry. In order to address that waste, organizations are moving to lean management because it exposes what and where these wastes are and rethink the way work is done via value streams.

Most providers are set up by departments, or vertical silos. In the case of manufacturing, it is products that traverse these departments, from receiving an order to collecting the money for it. In healthcare, what traverses departments are the patients.

Tracking patients horizontally through healthcare value stream changes the way you think about what is value-added and what is not. When you reconstruct patient flow through an experience at a clinic and you think horizontally; that is when you see all the waste.

I shall share with you below the eight different types of waste that inhibit patient flow, add cost, increase poor quality and infection and decrease patient and clinician satisfaction. When you remove waste, all these things change for the better. The value-added stream method is fundamental for patient flow in healthcare organizations.

1. Transportation

Transportation is entirely non-value-added. It contributes nothing to patient care. It adds to delays and increases likelihood there will be defects and dissatisfaction. Transportation includes moving patients from one department to the next, shifting supplies and equipment and moving instruments from sterile processing areas to the point of use and back again and even when patients travel to and from the actual hospital itself.

2. Inventory

Inventory can include pharmaceuticals, supplies, and patients, too, if you consider a waiting room in a hospital. The replenishment system should be based on use as opposed to some forecast. Only what is needed when it is needed is a good approach with inventory.

3. Unnecessary motions

Reaching, bending, twisting, and turning. These motions are all ergonomic issues abundant within healthcare. Clinicians are injured because processes like transporting a patient from wheelchairs to beds are not designed ergonomically. Staff takes time off for rehabilitation when unnecessary motions incapacitate them, which can result in a loss of productivity and enhance overall costs.

4. Waiting

Patients waiting for treatments, clinicians waiting for supplies as cliché as it sounds, time is money, and sometimes it is a matter of safety, too. There are some medications that need to be administered within a certain amount of time after a reaction or a procedure. Waiting can diminish the quality of the pharmaceutical and its effectiveness with the patient.

5. Overproducing

Overproducing is creating more of something than what is exactly needed. Sending medications to a patient's room that won't be used because the patient has already been discharged is an example. Along the same vein, this type of miscommunication between departments can also extend a patient's stay which is another form of overproduction. Other examples include repetition of diagnostic tests and the multiple registrations a patient has to endure when checking in. It's a laborious, unnecessary process and one time should be sufficient enough.

6. Processing Waste

Creating reports that don't get read or are not useful, administering duplicate tests; doing things where you produce 105 percent when you only needed to give 100 percent is processing waste.

7. Defects

There are countless defects within healthcare situations, such as hospital-acquired infections, early discharges that lead to readmissions, incomplete medical records or instrument kits in the emergency room and inaccurate medical billing. In many circumstances, these defects are covered-up through reworks and work-arounds, but with lean management, a light is shed on these defects, the root cause is figured out and a countermeasure is put in place that won't allow them to reoccur.

8. Unused human potential

With all the waste that already exists in healthcare, the last thing clinicians need to do is more non-value-added work, yet it happens all the time. Lean organizations involve people in redesigning work and real-time problem solving, unleashing human talent on the right things to solve problems and reduce waste for patients.

Chapter 7: A3 Problem-Solving Report

Toyota Motor Corporation is famed for its ability to relentlessly improve operational performance. Central to this ability is the training of engineers, supervisors and managers in a structured problem-solving approach that uses a tool called the A3 Problem-Solving Report.

The term "A3" derives from the paper size used for the report, which is the metric equivalent to 11" x 17" (or B-sized) paper. Toyota actually uses several styles of A3 reports for solving problems, for reporting project status, and for proposing policy changes; each having its own "storyline." I have focused on the problem-solving report simply because it is the most basic style, making it the best starting point.

Most problems that arise in organizations are addressed in superficial ways, what some call "first-order problem-solving." That is, we work around the problem to accomplish our immediate objective, but do not address the root causes of the problem so as to prevent its recurrence. By not addressing the root cause, we encounter the same problem or same type of problem again and again, and operational performance does not improve.

The A3 Process helps people engage in collaborative, in-depth problem-solving. It drives problem-solvers to address the root causes of problems which surface in day-to-day work routines. The A3 Process can be used for almost any situation, and our research has found that, when used properly (i.e., all of the steps are followed and completed), the chances of success improve dramatically.

The Seven A3 Problem Solving Steps in Detail

Using a very simple approach, A3 problem solving is composed of the following seven steps shown below.

Step 1: Background

In this step, you make the business case for selecting a particular problem for resolution. Upon your selection, clearly state how the problem impacts the strategic business objectives around customers, process, financials, new products, etc.

Step 2: Problem Statement

Detail the specifics of the problem. These may include the magnitude of the problem, where and when the problem occurred, and the problem's impact on the business. By defining these specifics on a quantitative scale, you help to bring the problem to life for your organization.

Step 3: Goal Statement

In this step, state what you are trying to accomplish by initiating the A3 problem solving project. Map out what goals you are trying to achieve and set a timeframe for completing these goals.

Step 4: Root Cause Analysis

Having fully defined the problem, carry out a root cause analysis to determine the most basic reasons of your problem. Be as thorough as possible.

Step 5: Countermeasures

With the root causes in place, come up with the countermeasures that you will use to reach your objective in solving the problem. Draw up a detailed plan that outlines who will deploy the countermeasures and when this deployment will be completed.

Step 6: Effect Confirmation

Having implemented the countermeasures, look at the results. Determine whether the results indicate that your countermeasures were effective in meeting your objective.

Step 7: Follow Up Action

Having achieved your results, deploy the infrastructure for sustaining the gains (such as standardization, audits, dashboards and reviews). Make sure that you roll out your findings across the organization, which in Japanese is called yoko-narabi-tenkai, meaning "lateral deployment of findings to other groups."

A3 problem solving may appear to be a simple seven step approach which helps in solving business problems. However, it is not that simple.

Chapter 8: Using Five Whys in Healthcare Environment

By repeatedly asking the question 'why?' (Use five as a rule of thumb), you can peel away the layers of an issue, just like the layers of an onion, which can lead you to the root cause of a problem. The reason for a problem can often lead into another question; you may need to ask the question fewer or more than five times before you get to the origin of a problem.

The real key is to avoid assumptions and logic traps and encourage the team to keep drilling down to the real root cause.

When does it work best?

By quickly identifying the source of an issue or problem, you can focus resources in the correct areas and ensure that you are tackling the true cause of the issue, not just its symptoms.

How to complete the five whys
1. Write down the specific problem. Writing it down helps you formalise the problem and describe it accurately. It also helps a team focus on the same problem.
2. Use brainstorming to ask why the problem occurs then, write the answer down.
3. If this answer doesn't identify the source of the problem, ask 'why?' again and write that answer down.

4. Loop back to step three until the team agrees that they have identified the problem's root cause. Again, this may take fewer or more than five 'whys?'

Why use the five whys?

- Helps you to identify the root causes of a problem.
- Helps you to determine the relationship between different root causes of a problem.
- It is one of the simplest analysis tools as it's easy to complete without statistical analysis.
- It is easy to learn and apply.

Five whys and cause and effect diagrams

The five whys can be used independently or as a part of a cause and effect diagram. The diagram helps you explore all potential or real causes which result in a failure or problem. Once you have established all the inputs on the cause and effect diagram, you can use the five whys technique to drill down to the root causes.

Tips

Moving into 'fix-it' mode too quickly might mean dealing with symptoms but leaving the problem unresolved, so use the five whys to ensure that the cause of the problem is being addressed.

If you don't ask the right questions, you don't get the right answers. A question asked in the right way often points to its own answer.

Example 1

- The patient was late in theatre, it caused a delay. Why?
- There was a long wait for a trolley. Why?
- A replacement trolley had to be found. Why?
- The original trolley's safety rail was worn and had eventually broken. Why?
- It had not been regularly checked for wear. Why?

The root cause - there is no equipment maintenance schedule. Setting up a proper maintenance schedule helps ensure that patients should never again be late due to faulty equipment. This reduces delays and improves flow. If you simply repair the trolley or do a one-off safety rail check, the problem may happen again sometime in the future.

Example 2

- The patient's diagnosis of skin cancer was considerably delayed. Why?
- The excision biopsy report was not seen by the surgeon. Why?
- The report was filed in the patient's notes without being seen by the surgeon. Why?
- It was the receptionist job to do the filing. Why?
- The junior doctors were busy with other tasks. Why?

The root cause - that the doctors' other tasks were seen as more important than filing. The system has now been changed. A copy of all biopsy reports is now sent to the consultant surgeon responsible for the patient and no reports are filed unless they have been signed by a doctor.

What next?

You may find that you will identify the root cause of the issue identified. The next suggested step is to complete a cause and effect diagram.

Brainstorming to help you to identify potential solutions to the cause identified.

You will need to communicate the outcomes to others to ensure that the root cause of the problem is understood and that everyone is focused on working on the correct problem area, not treating its symptoms.

Chapter 9: How to Use Value Stream Maps in Healthcare

Value stream mapping (VSM) can help you map, visualize, and understand the flow of patients, materials (e.g., bags of screened blood or plasma), and information. The "value stream" is all of the actions required to complete a particular process, and the goal of VSM is to identify improvements that can be made to reduce waste (e.g., patient wait times).

How is VSM applied to healthcare?

When used within healthcare, one obvious application for VSM is mapping a patient's path to treatment to improve service and minimize delays. To accurately map a system, obtaining high-quality, reliable data about the flow of information and the time a patient spends at or between steps is key. Accurately timing process steps and using multi-departmental teams is essential to obtain a true picture of what is going on.

To map a patient's path to treatment, a current state map can be created in a VSM tool to act as a baseline and to identify areas for improvement.

Current State Value Stream Map

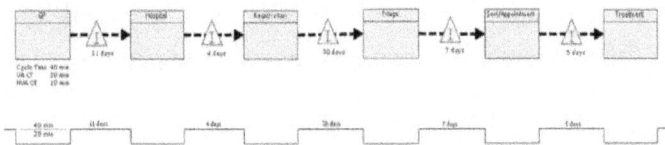

For example, the first step a patient takes is to visit his general Practitioner "GP", and this is represented as a rectangular process shape in the VSM. The time the patient spends at this step can be broken down into value-added ("VA") and non value-added ("NVA") cycle times. VA is time the customer is willing to pay for: that is, the 20 minutes spent consulting with the GP. NVA is the time the customer is not willing to pay for, i.e., the 20 minutes spent in the waiting room before the appointment.

The dotted line arrow between process steps is called a push arrow. This shows that once a patient completes a step, they are "pushed" to the next step. This is inefficient, and a more efficient process can be designed by changing push steps to continuous flow or "pull" steps. The yellow triangles indicate the time a patient spends waiting for the next process. These steps are a non-value added action for the patient.

By identifying all of the steps, you can start to map the whole process out, moving from left to right. Once you have mapped out the entire system, an ideal future state map can be created, and possibly a series of future states in between. These can identify areas for improvement, and once implemented, they can become the "new" current state map.

How do you improve the current state map?

When looking for areas of improvement, try to focus on changes to improve the flow of patients through the process. Continuous flow is the ideal and moves patients through the system without them having to wait. However, continuous flow is not always possible, so instead other changes might be introduced such as first-in first-out (FIFO).

Also be sure to take a look at the takt time, which can help you decipher the pace of customer demand. In this case, takt time can be interpreted as the number of patients that can be treated per unit of time.

Once you have completed the current and future state maps, you can compare the two, quantify improvement opportunities, and look at how to implement the changes. In this example, the triage and sort/appointment steps might be combined so that fewer visits to the hospital were required by the patient and they receive treatment faster.

Chapter 10: Lean Mistake Proofing Through Source Checks

In Healthcare, we do lots of audits. Audits require inspection. But, did you know that each inspection is only about 80% effective? Audits may not be concurrent and are sometimes very after-the-fact. It is difficult to provide timely, accurate feedback to change outcomes when we are auditing the process so after-the-fact. It is also very difficult, if not impossible, to find the root cause of the problem after some time has passed.

By using source and self-checks, we can prevent errors at the start of a process and defects in outcomes. Successive checks shorten the feedback loop. By utilizing this concept, there are redundancies that can correct errors at the source and immediately as the process is taking place instead of providing feedback at some later time. But wait a minute this all sounds like WASTE! In fact, it is a form of waste. However, until we have eliminated all of the causes of errors in a process, it is each supplier's responsibility to deliver DEFECT-FREE service to their internal customers. Therefore, in Lean, we accept these temporary countermeasures until we find permanent solutions to the causes.

One obvious example of source, self and successive checks is implementation of the Universal Protocol to prevent wrong person and wrong site/side surgeries.

The redundancies may seem annoying, however you can begin to see that the 20% ineffectiveness of audits is overcome by the successive checks, by checking everything at the source and doing your own self-checks.

Looking at the drawing, the person in operation "A," begins the process by first inspecting everything at the source; are all necessary elements/materials present at the start? If not, the self-check provides immediate feedback that something needs to be corrected.

As the process is handed off, the person in operation "B," begins their part of the process by inspecting everything from their source; are all necessary elements/materials present for their part of the process? If not, they can and should provide immediate feedback to Supplier A. Customer/Supplier B does a self-check of their work and prepares to handoff to Customer/Supplier "C," who does the same.

This is why we do it, even if it feels like we do the same thing multiple times! Do those successive and, yes, sometimes redundant checks. If there is an error or issue, provide timely feedback to your source. This is how we achieve 100% percent inspection of the process and move toward 100% quality while relentlessly working to eliminate root causes.

Chapter 11: Using the 5s Lean Tool for Healthcare

Lean is a problem-solving approach for continuous improvement and the 5s tool is of value in health care settings.

Healthcare costs are increasing more rapidly than costs for other products and services. Healthcare providers, particularly hospitals, are under significant pressure to reduce costs while at the same time improving service and patient safety, reducing patient waiting times, and minimizing errors and associated litigation. However, most hospitals are not making the necessary improvements in cost, quality, and safety.

A report by the UK NHS Office of Inspector General finds that 20 percent of consecutive inpatient stays were associated with poor quality care, unnecessary fragmentation of care, or both. Healthcare organizations, historically, have not been designed to make service processes or a "value stream" of care flow. Healthcare services often use a "batch and queue" process, with patients spending the bulk of their time waiting until a healthcare professional is ready (i.e., push versus pull with regard to service delivery). Patient cycle time (the total time from the beginning to the end of a process) in our hospitals, laboratories, and therapy settings becomes a key measurement that needs to improve.

Why use Lean Tools in Healthcare?

All types of organizations are leveraging Lean principles and tools. Many organizations are trying to function effectively in the face of growing challenges such as a high costs, declining market share, and limited capacity. In all of these cases, Lean can have an immediate, positive impact on business.

Healthcare organizations are made up of a series of processes with diverse services or lines of business. Therefore, you need to build delivery systems with these lines of business in mind.

Using Lean Thinking, your organization can achieve a number of benefits, which may include improved quality, increased operational flexibility, reduced cycle time within processes, more efficient use of space, consistent service delivery, reduced lead-times, and reduced operating costs.

Lean Tools: 5s

Lean tools grew out of the need to have mechanisms in place to support the lean way of thinking and to allow flow to permeate a process. Value stream mapping, 5s, Poka Yoke, and Kanban are among the most popular Lean tools.

The five components of 5s are defined as sort, set in order, shine, standardize, and sustain.

5s is a method that reduces waste in your work environment through better workplace organization, visual communication, and general cleanliness. This is one of the primary tools necessary to improve your processes by eliminating wastes such as motion, searching, inventory (queuing) and improve quality and functionality within all departments.

5s Benefits

5s drives a cleaner work environment and organizes the workplace. It is a Lean tool that should be implemented along with process improvements identified when value-stream mapping your business processes. When implementing 5s, you rapidly affect your work or production environment with a minimal expenditure. Most organizations report 15-20% efficiency improvement in several months, which is sustainable over time. 5s provides some of the following benefits:

- A cleaner workplace for enhanced safety and reduced clutter.
- An organized, efficient workplace for increased productivity.
- An always-ready environment that fosters and promotes compliance with regulatory standards.
- The reduction of inventory and supply costs.
- The recapture of valuable space and minimizing overhead costs.
- The impact of "how we feel" about our workplace, organization, and ourselves.

There will be somebody who habitually expresses contrary opinions that may argue that their messiness is beneficial to them; some point to the fact that time spent keeping their environment organized distracts from the important things in their jobs like time analyzing or thinking and defining new approaches to care.

However, they miss the point; truly organized people are not organized just for the sake of order. Instead, their organization is a result of having a process to manage all of the things in their lives.

These folks avoid interment in paper or e-mails in their inbox by having a clear approach for handling all of the responsibilities in their lives. By managing things effectively, they avoid clutter and chaos.

How to Begin Thinking About 5s

When implementing 5s, staff should not focus on getting organized. Rather, they need to consider how they deal with all the things that come to them and what is within their environment; this will help in creating a 5s workplace.

For example, doctors do not focus on getting their operating room organized. Instead, they have a defined process for preparing for an operation; they wash their hands in a certain way; the instruments used are predefined and laid out in a specific way.

Instruments are checked and counted in a standard way for each surgical case every day. The result of these processes is a 5s workplace.

Let us use the practical example of cleaning your garage to understand how you would implement 5s in the workplace.

The first step that you do when cleaning your garage is open the door, back out the cars, and pull everything out that is lying around. You then make piles of the things you will keep, what you will sell in the neighbourhood garage sale, items you need to return to a neighbour, what to donate, and what to discard.

This first step in the process is called **"Sort."**

The next step is to put away the things that you wish to keep. However, this time you will put them in a specific location: "A place for everything and everything in its place." You make a shadow board for your tools. This will allow you and others to look at the board in the future and know exactly what location to return the tool to, and you can easily identify missing tools by the shape of the empty space on the board. More importantly it allows you to find your tools when needed. You install hooks for bicycles in the ceiling joints and clamps for brooms and shovels. This step in the process is called **"Set in order."**

With everything sorted and set in order, it is time to clean the entire garage. When you are cleaning, you observe things that need to be fixed, such as the cracked switch plate and the torn weather stripping on the utility door. You repair these things so that they do not become a bigger problem, cause damage, or put a family member's safety at risk. Further, you hose down the garage floor and remove oil spills with a degreasing agent. This step is called **"Shine."**

Now you can stand back and look at your accomplishment. The garage looks great. Everything is clean and organized; you can actually find what you are looking for in the garage. However, beware you will need to repeat this exercise again in a few months because you did not **"Standardize" and "Sustain"** your efforts.

Standardizing means to create the guidelines for Sort, Set in order, and Shine and then to actually follow those guidelines.

Sustain is having the discipline and keeping the 5s processes going.

By implementing all of the 5s components, you have transformed your garage into a neat, orderly, and safe place. Everyone can find things quickly, and you can easily recognize when something is missing.

This simple example reveals the power of 5s and the importance of using all of the 5s steps to move your Lean efforts forward.

5s Summary

1. **Sort:** Remove those items (unnecessary supplies, equipment, and junk) that you do not need to do the job. This will remove

clutter, free up floor space, and aid in improving workspace efficiency.

2. **Set in order:** Have a place for everything and everything is kept in its place. Place items in proximity (point of use) to make the caregiver's job easier. Label and identify the exact location for equipment and supplies to make this easy to maintain.

3. **Shine:** Sorted and straightened areas are easier to keep clean. Shine, another word for "scrubbing and cleaning," is important to everyone, not to mention making patients and their families feel they are intrusting their lives to an organization that values cleanliness.

4. **Standardize:** You must standardize regular maintenance and upkeep of the 5s process. It is essential to be deliberate in your ongoing efforts and to create guidelines for sort, set in order, and shine.

5. **Sustain:** The true value of the 5s process is to sustain your customer/patient and Joint Commission ready approach at all times. Use simple but effective audit processes to accomplish this. Sustaining is the most important "S," and it requires the most discipline.

How to Begin Using Lean Tools

First, remember that no single Lean tool will be effective alone or sustain a Lean initiative. Lean is a problem-solving approach to eliminate waste and increase efficiency by creating flow and allowing pull along a service value stream, and thereby creating value for the patient. Simply cleaning up the workplace environment in isolation will not achieve the objectives of Lean Thinking.

Commitment and support for lean initiatives must come from top executive management, however, even more critical, from the "bottom up" for implementation. Decision-making and value stream improvements must be pushed down to the lowest levels of your organization.

Consultants are frequently engaged as Lean change agents rather than as facilitators and mentors. Your staff should be educated to lead and must be actively involved in any Lean implementation. The people best equipped to understand the work environment, issues, challenges, what will work, and what won't are the folks doing the work every day. Empowering and educating your staff is essential to achieve sustainable and continuous daily improvement that ensures long-term success for Lean Thinking in your organization.

Look for and engage consultants who collaborate with you and present an implementation approach that educates, facilitates, and mentors you and your staff. Ultimately, the consultant should become an advisor to your organization, with your staff assuming leadership and execution of the majority of your Lean implementation.

Healthcare organization can leverage Lean Thinking and its tools to identify and eliminate waste and thereby increase efficiency with minimal cost and realize tremendous benefits.

Chapter 12: Other Lean Tool for Healthcare

1. Kaizen

Kaizen an integral part of the Lean Healthcare philosophy, is a Japanese word that means to make peoples jobs easier by taking them apart, studying them and making improvements. The intent is to make people more productive by improving their working environment and the focus is immediate action rather than longer-term alternatives to change. Kaizen is also known as the Deliberate Application of Common Sense.

Improvement begins with the admission that every organization has problems and these problems provide opportunities for change and improvement. The traditional conventional wisdom holds that "If it is not broke, don't fix it." The Kaizen philosophy takes the view that every process can be improved and therefore even if you think "It is not broke, fix it anyway."

The best knowledge resides with the people who actually perform the work. They know the problems and often the solutions. During a Kaizen event, they make the recommendations on how to improve the process and they make the physical changes to the processes. They will also support and continue the process after the event is over.

Because the people who have to live with the processes on a daily basis are the people who study the current process, design the improved process and then physically make the changes to convert to the new process, there is tremendous involvement, buy-in and ownership of the improvements. The changes created through the Kaizen event are very sustainable. The processes do not revert back to the less efficient way of doing things.

One of the Key Concepts of Kaizen is that "If there is No Action there can be No Success." The goal is not a 100% solution that solves all the problems at one time. But rather a 60% solution that can be accomplished in a one-week time frame with the intent to hold another event in several months that further improves the processes. The process does not have to be perfect the first time. Strive for "base hits" not "home runs" and no idea is a bad idea. Just do it!

Quick and simple is better than slow and fancy. Be creative; get the new process in place and working. Utilize what exists to implement the new process quickly. A Kaizen event is not a license to spend and should be accomplished with very little expenditure. The essence of Kaizen is making improvements with what you have (or less) using existing people, machines, computers, space, etc. Overall emphasis is placed on creating solutions and improvements with existing assets. As a result, they are a very cost-effective method to create dramatic improvements in processes.

A typical Kaizen event is one week long. A team is usually a cross-functional team that is composed of from 8 to 10 people. The team is composed of people who are in the process to be reviewed, such as the nurses, lead people, and supervisors. Additional resources from other departments are assigned to support the event. Even personnel from suppliers or Doctors can be included.

2. Poka Yoke (Mistake Proofing)

Japanese term that means mistake proofing. To avoid (yokeru) inadvertent errors (poka).

A Poka Yoke device is one that prevents incorrect parts of a process from being worked or easily identifies a flaw or error.

- Any method that can help caregivers or operators avoid mistakes
- The Lean Healthcare concept recognizes that the optimal location to prevent or correct mistakes is at the point of creation of the problem.
- Late recognition of a mistake or defect is never as efficient and typically has a cumulative effect.

Poka-yoke - 'mistake-proofing', a means of providing visual or other signals to indicate a characteristic state. Often referred to as 'error-proofing', poke-yoke is actually the first step in truly error-proofing a system. Error proofing is a technique of preventing errors by designing the process, equipment, and tools so that a procedure literally cannot be performed incorrectly.

Mistake Proofing Philosophy

- Believes that a zero defect process is possible when using Lean Healthcare tools.
- Promotes defect prevention vs. defect detection.
- Recognizes that people forget and make errors; also machines/processes fail and make errors.
- Respect the intelligence of workers by taking the judgment out of repetitive tasks where errors are likely to occur.
- Utilizes people working in the process to mistake proof the work because they own the process.

3. Set-Up or Changeover Reduction (SMED)

Set-up and changeover reduction is a valuable tool utilized in the Lean Healthcare effort to decrease overall costs and bottlenecks. Set-up or "change-over" is defined as the time required from the completion of the last until the start of the nest procedure. Set-up includes getting instruments, getting supplies, setting-up rooms, getting materials, and getting paperwork. This entire process can take place in less than 10 minutes!

The SMED process focuses on reduction of setup and changeover time as a way of improving utilization, increasing capacity and more volume. Changeover of rooms or equipment can be accomplished in less time and serves as a goal for change.

Benefits of a set-up / change-over reduction or SMED program include:

- Reduction of inventory in supplies and instruments.
- Dramatic reduction in flow time.
- Elimination of waste and non value-added operations.
- Improvement of capacity and volume.
- Increase in flexibility.
- Improvement in cash flow through reduction of inventory, waste, and rapid transfer of information to speed the patient flow process.
- Increase in competitiveness.
- Increase in Patient Satisfaction.
- Increase in Doctor Satisfaction.

Chapter 13: Optimize Healthcare's Procurement Strategies

Procurement cost accounts for more than 30 percent of a hospitals' expenditure, in fact it is the largest financial outlay second only to staffing, and yet many healthcare institutions relegate its management to the back office.

Below are five key points that will help any hospital lean and improve its procurement function.

- Make the move from transactional to strategic sourcing.
- Employ people with a commercial background.
- Address procurement at an executive level.
- Focus on clinical engagement.
- Don't compromise on patient care.

Commonly, the first thing hospital executives will look at when they are losing money is staffing levels, however that method of leaning your institution is limited and often leads of compromised patient care. What hospital executives should be addressing first and foremost is the procurement function.

Transactional Versus Strategic Sourcing

Typically what we find is this is an area that is not been particularly well managed. The typical procurement function is very transactional; the department is placing purchase orders, monitoring arrivals, and distributing goods, but they are not actually doing any proactive sourcing, they are not driving out cost savings. We find that many procurement departments are transactional rather than strategic.

If you took a snapshot of a typical hospital procurement function you would label it 'back office'. You would probably find the department in a porter-cabin at the back of the hospital, titled, 'Supplies' rather than 'Procurement' and furthermore a team of people who are not very senior or indeed commercial would most likely run it.

Clinical Engagement

We find the key to success when it comes to hospital procurement is clinical engagement. The procurement function doesn't interact with the front line staff; they don't interact with the clinicians, the nurses or head of estates; they are in the back office managing transactions. To this end it is essential to have very good commercial people heading up the department, who work closely with clinicians. If you can achieve this, you can make some extremely impressive savings.

Take an orthopaedics department as an example, it requires a very specialised segment of spend. It is the surgeons and clinicians who have the specialised knowledge about technology and products so in order to make cost savings you have got to work very closely with those people. You have got to understand their exact requirements and then it is the procurement function's role to fully understand the market. If you merge both expertise and work very closely with one another you can source the best value suppliers and arrangements for the department.

It is vital for the procurement function to work alongside the clinical arm of the hospital. The only way to make significant cost savings is to work out all the possible commercial options and to teach clinicians to understand the commercial implications of their decisions.

What we often find is that the clinical staff are making decisions regarding procurement, and they are making those decisions without any cost knowledge or commercial understanding. The procurement function should be doing this for them; it should be the conduit for innovation, they should be working with the supply base, to bring innovative products and solutions to the hospital. Instead the suppliers go straight to the clinicians, and it's a bit like a kid going into a toy shop; of course they want the best, newest products, however it should be the role of procurement to educate and negotiate on behalf of the clinical staff to ensure they get the products they need, while also managing cost base. Healthcare Procurement strategies should be on the boardroom agenda

Focus on Patient Outcome

Not compromising patient outcome is very simple, procurement should be getting best value for the hospital, and it's not only about cost. It has to take into consideration all factors including quality and outcome, as well as safety. Before you undertake any work on the category of business spend you must understand the business requirements so again it comes back to clinical engagement, you must spend lots of time with the stakeholder understanding what they need now and in the future. If you understand that you can then procure against it; you will select suppliers against what is required by the hospital and you will search for the best commercial option. It is simply no good to source the lowest cost product, because it may not tick all the boxes for the department. This haphazard approach to procurement could in fact end up costing you more money in the long term.

Within the healthcare industry there are lots of collaborative procurement hubs; regional focused buying organisations however there is a fairly big questions mark over how effective these are. Collaboration is great and there is a theory that says the more you can bundle together in terms of volume, the more attractive it is to a supplier, and the lower cost you get, however, it is hard enough to get surgeons within one hospital to agree on what they want, let alone surgeons across many hospitals.

When it comes to cost saving, commitment is key. What we have found is that many hospitals can get better prices, by being able to commit to the buyers that they have selected. It is a mix, logic says collaboration and volume should trump anything else but in practice it is not necessarily true.

Employing the Right People

It may be cliché to say, but employing the right team of people within the procurement function is probably the most important factor when it comes to efficiency and cost saving. You have got to have good people. Strategic sourcing, proactively driving savings requires good people; it requires commercial people and people who are able to manage the supply market, internal stakeholders and business requirements. They must be able to work peer to peer with the CEO or the Head of Orthopaedics or the Chief Nurse.

There has not been enough emphasis put on the procurement department as a key function, it has been neglected. The procurement function is seen as a low-level function that reports into finance, so it has no executive visibility. Procurement is generally not on the executive agenda and it should be. It is fundamental, procurement should be on the board level, without doubt, and you need good people to do that. The procurement function should have a very high profile within the hospital; it should be one of the backbones of the organisation.

Chapter 14: Optimize Healthcare's Supply Chain Strategies

Healthcare supply chains can account for up to 50 percent of expenditure, which is why it is absolutely essential for executives to sit up and take notice. In order to run a successful operation, administrators need to ensure the supply chain is totally efficient.

1. Involve doctors in supply chain discussions especially related to doctor's preference items (PPIs).

PPIs (proton pump inhibitors) account for an estimated 40 percent of a typical supply budget, however they can also cause tension between administration and doctors. Every year, medical device companies introduce new models of high-end, implantable devices such as pacemakers, artificial knees and spinal discs. But while the new model nearly always arrives with a higher price tag, there is often little data to suggest it is a clinical improvement over the incumbent.

One way to address this is through value analysis committees comprised of doctors, materials representatives and administration that evaluate PPI selection. If clinicians want to acquire a new PPI, they have to present evidence-based, clinically sound information suggesting the new device would provide a safer or more effective result to a committee of key decision makers.

By aligning doctors with administrators, supply chain managers and other leaders, and by taking a data-driven approach, health systems can limit the acquisition of new, costlier products to just those where data clearly shows increased value.

2. Make sure the entire operation is efficient, including the seemingly 'insignificant' costs.

For many providers, there are multiple opportunities to reduce costs by addressing so-called 'low-hanging fruit'. This could be as simple as replacing branded items with non-branded ones for example. Other options include ensuring that all care sites within a health system are buying identical products using the same contract. This concept of product standardization can be extended to a regional or national level via participation in a group purchasing organization. While these opportunities may not result in huge savings individually, they do in aggregate, and uncovering them isn't resource-intensive.

3. Optimize product utilization for cost effectiveness.

Optimizing product utilization can be a complicated process however it can produce big savings. Hospitals use comparative data that allows them to make decisions based on quality and cost, they can also gain an understanding of which products are top performers nationwide.

4. Don't underestimate energy efficiency opportunities when it comes to saving money.

Energy costs consume up to three percent of a hospital's total operating budget and at least 15 percent of their annual profits, reports suggest. Efficient energy use is an often-overlooked opportunity to reduce cost, increase net profits and contribute to the bottom line and is often as simple as replacing energy inefficient light bulbs.

5. Remember to address 'dead stock'

Second to labour costs, supplies are the largest expense for most health systems. Reducing on-hand inventory value and increasing inventory efficiency can present significant savings opportunities.

Managing Hospital Supply Chain Efficiency

As mention at the beginning of this chapter; believe it or not, supply chain activities account for approximately 50 percent of hospital budgets when you factor in the cost of the goods, procurement, storage, engineering, pharmacy, food service and nurses' time spent on supply chain activities. It's no wonder then that supply chain management should be a top priority for hospital CEOs, but unbelievably many don't consider the supply chain from a strategic perspective.

The economic downturn has had a positive effect in this respect, giving supply chain management a renewed prominence, boosting it in many hospitals from the basement to the executive suite and organisations that have placed strategic focus on the discipline are reaping significant savings. But there are still a lot of changes that can be made to streamline hospital supply chains and it is necessary considering that by 2020, medical supplies will surpass labour as the biggest expense for hospitals and health systems. Where to Start

- Standardise commodities.
- Maximise use of contracts with group purchasing organisations.
- Manage inventory.
- Use relationships with vendors to the fullest extent.

By addressing the tasks above, hospitals and health systems will immediately recognise significant savings. However, the biggest opportunity lies in resource utilisation and reducing variation in care. You cannot sacrifice quality for cost. For that reason you should not base your decisions solely on cost. In some cases, the higher cost item is associated with better outcomes. If we can reduce length of stay, eliminate infections and speed recovery time, we are impacting the bottom line in a big way.

With this in mind it is also essential that physicians are involved in the decision making process to both enhance their understanding and to receive valuable input on care delivery processes.

Key Steps to Effective Supply Chain Management

Whoever can deliver care at the highest quality and the lowest cost will be the winner. The key steps below will help CEOs manage strategic supply chain and gain the best return on investment.

1. Build Relationships

As a supply chain officer it is important to understand that you don't know everything. Building relationships with colleagues, both clinical and non-clinical throughout the organisation and listening to their feedback will help make the supply chain more efficient and workable long term.

2. Align with Doctors

Organisations need to engage doctors proactively in supply chain management. By placing them in leadership positions on value-analysis committees can help achieve significant buy-in from medical staff. They also have the technical know-how and can thus be involved in contract negotiations, formulary development and technology assessment.

3. Practice Evidence-Based Medicine

Eliminating variations in care through the adoption of evidence-based medicine not only improves outcomes, but also reduces expenses. Reducing readmissions and preventing infections, among other

79

things, optimizes reimbursement and places less pressure on the supply chain.

4.   Focus on Clinical Integration

The supply chain should be integrated with the care delivery process. A high-performing supply chain delivers the right product, at the right time, in the right quantity, at the right cost, resulting in improved outcomes and greater efficiency.

5.   Automate the Supply Chain

The need for automation in the supply chain is clear. Lack of automation can lead to overstock and overspending on supplies. Materials management information systems provide real-time information on pricing, product availability, contract compliance and usage. Automation also enhances supply chain accuracy and expedites the billing process.

6.   Adopt Standards

The adoption of supply chain standards such as GS1 (Global Standards One) can enhance efficiency, patient safety and regulatory compliance.

7.   Enhance Value Analysis

The value analysis process helps hospitals determine whether they are getting the right product at the right prices. Value analysis teams provide nurses, physicians and others a say in product utilization and performance.

8. Think Lean

Process improvement methodologies, such as Lean and Six Sigma, can identify inefficiencies within the supply chain and streamline processes.

Chapter 15: Lean Thinking in Healthcare

Lean in healthcare is organization's cultural commitment to applying the scientific method to designing, performing, and continuously improving the work delivered by teams of people, leading to measurably better value for patients and other stakeholders.

Below are six principles of Lean to help healthcare leaders consider implementing Lean or assess their current state of Lean implementation.

1. **Lean is an attitude of continuous improvement.** Lean involves a culture of continuous improvement in which leaders are always raising the bar to drive value.

2. **Lean is value-creating.** The ultimate goal of Lean is to improve value. When measuring improvement from Lean interventions, healthcare leaders should always compare benefits and burdens.

3. **Lean is unity of purpose.** Lean can unify teams around a shared goal.

4. **Lean is respect for the people who do the work.** Healthcare leaders need to empower front-line workers to drive improvement.

5. **Lean is visual.** Visual tracking centres provide easy access to data and serve as a place for communicating concerns and new ideas.

6. **Lean is flexible regimentation.** In a Lean approach, workers need to identify root causes of problems and change standards to optimize processes.

Tips on Adapting Manufacturing Based Lean Strategies to Healthcare

As mentioned earlier in this book the Lean model of process improvement originated in Japan with the Toyota Production System. Many hospitals and health systems have found the model's principles of eliminating non-value added activity and streamlining processes useful in improving efficiency in healthcare. However, hospitals may need to adapt some of Lean's practices to align more closely with hospital operations and culture.

Below are tips on translating Lean strategies to a healthcare environment.

1. **Lead with patient benefit.** Hospitals have a patient-centric culture, and as such, proposals for change need to focus on the benefits to the patient. To gain buy-in and engage staff and clinicians, Lean leaders need to base improvement projects on helping patients first. The benefits to the patient can then ultimately translate into greater efficiency and cost savings.

Instead of the historic path in industry where energy is more on the cost element, in healthcare it has to be more on the patient, caregivers and how a project translates into value.

2. **Pilot first.** The traditional Lean approach to improvement is "ready, aim, fire," we changed this approach to "ready, controlled fire, aim, fire." Under this method, an improvement team plans a pilot project (ready), executes the pilot (controlled fire), makes adjustments to the intervention (aim) and deploys it system-wide (fire).

This approach allows Lean leaders to learn about the hospital's or department's culture before instituting a change across the entire organization.

3. **Time is medicine.** In hospitals, time is medicine. When working with doctors and other clinicians in an improvement team, Lean leaders need to plan meetings in advance so doctors do not feel the Lean project is an intrusion on their patient care. While in manufacturing team members may be readily available for improvement projects, healthcare providers may need more notice before participating.

For example, in the past we had to plan doctors' involvement in a Lean project a month in advance to allow the doctors to adjust their schedules so patient care is not interrupted.

Chapter 16: Lean Healthcare in Action

Excessive wait times in a hospital can be a source of great frustration for patients, which affects their level of satisfaction with the hospital. Since hospitals will be held more accountable for their scores on the Hospital Consumer Assessment of Healthcare Providers and Systems survey, they will need to improve things like waiting times to ensure patients are satisfied.

In 2010, outpatient chemotherapy patients at our local hospital's Cancer Institute had to wait from one to two hours to receive treatment after checking in. This long wait time influenced not only patient satisfaction, but also employee satisfaction, as employees' goal is to deliver care to patients when needed. In addition, the extensive waiting period often caused patients to become vocal and animated about their frustration with the providers.

1. **Multi-disciplinary team.** To solve this problem, our local hospital continuous improvement team developed a multi-disciplinary team including administrator, the chemotherapy unit leader, doctors, nurses, laboratory technicians and pharmacists. This chemotherapy wait team analyzed the current process of treating patients to identify areas of inefficiency.

One of the keys to the success of the intervention was the team members' collaboration. Clinicians and staff working together to provide care is a different dynamic than working together to solve process problems. Just because people are a team in care delivery doesn't mean they are a cohesive team when solving problems using Lean or other problem-solving techniques. The leaders, staff and clinicians in the chemotherapy unit needed to understand each other's roles and work together to effectively identify areas of non-value added activity and develop solutions.

2. **Registration.** One area of inefficiency the team identified was how patients were checked in and taken to rooms for treatment. Initially, the first available nurse would take the first patient who signs in to his or her room. The process was not formal or organized, and it created delays.

The improvement team changed this process by developing schedule templates that assign nurse navigators to specific patients on the schedule. The nurses guide patients through their treatment, improving both efficiency and patients' experience. In addition, the team established team leaders in the unit to address any bottlenecks in patient flow.

3. **Scheduling.** Another area the hospital's chemotherapy wait team addressed was scheduling. Originally, the chemotherapy schedules did not account for the length of treatment for each patient. Depending on the patient's condition, treatment may last anywhere from one to four hours. The team created new schedules that enabled staff to optimize scheduling for long and short treatments

4. **Lab.** To speed treatment, the hospital moved the lab equipment from outside the building to the floor above the chemotherapy unit. The physical proximity of these departments speeds turnaround time for lab results, preventing delays and backups.

5. **Pharmacy and Doctors Orders.** The chemotherapy team shared the unit's schedule with the pharmacists to ensure they would have the correct medication for patients on time. The team also paired nurses with doctors to ensure each patient receives the correct medication and dosage.

In addition, the unit worked to improve the completeness of doctors' pharmacy orders. Sometimes orders for patients' medication would be absent, missing a signature or have the incorrect medication. Initially, roughly 15 percent of doctors' orders had at least one problem. By tracking each doctor's rate of incomplete orders and posting these rates visibly, unit nurse managers motivated doctors to improve. The nurse managers also reviewed the rates regularly with doctors to help them reduce the rate of problem orders.

6. **Leadership.** Reports on patients' wait times in the chemotherapy unit are reviewed at several levels of the organization, from the frontline workers to the heads of the department all the way to the CEO. Having key measures at every level of the organization and having a focus on it consistently has allowed the short wait time to sustain itself.

Outcomes for patients and providers

Through these efforts, the chemotherapy wait team reduced the wait time for chemotherapy patients from two hours to 35 minutes to 20 minutes and eventually less than 20 minutes. Ongoing changes and process evaluation caused these incremental reductions, enabling the unit to continue making progress.

The Lean improvement project also benefited the providers' relationships. They start to understand the demands and expectations of each other and the creation of commitments upstream and downstream. There was a strengthened comprehension of what each person does and respect for what each person does.

They continued with their lean journey by using various Kaizen approach to help them identify opportunities quicker and react in a quicker fashion.

This hospital has a team of four senior people with a variety of Lean and engineering backgrounds plus an expanding rota of analytical support staff charged with continuously identifying opportunities to improve performance. The group looks at everything from quality measures like infection rates and pressure ulcers to measurable outside quality areas such as how fast a blood specimen gets from the clinical area to the central lab. "The impact this team has had is amazing. Getting different multidisciplinary teams around the table to understand interdependencies and where bottlenecks are provides solutions.

Kaizen (Japanese for good change) projects are three to five days breakthrough events:
1. Standardize an operation and activities.
2. Measure the operation (find cycle time and amount of in-process inventory).
3. Gauge measurements against requirements.
4. Innovate to meet requirements and increase productivity.
5. Standardize the new, improved operations.
6. Continue cycle ad infinitum.

The Kaizen approach is not a one-and-done strategy. You have really; truly believe in continuous process improvement. They continue to look for opportunities to be more efficient, more responsible, more friendly for patients and focus on quality initiatives. There is no limitation to the areas where you can use Lean principles.

One effort has focused on improving the patient experience in ambulatory sites. They look at the process of the patient from the moment he or she arrives until the moment he or she leaves and eliminate non-value-added experiences. Are patients waiting too long? Are they getting all the information they should be provided with? However an additional challenge is the ability to measure patient experiences "because it's very difficult to improve something you cannot measure. The measures are not always perfect but at least they are directional.

In one ambulatory site, the hospital team reduced registration time by 60 percent and patient wait-time from registration to doctor interaction by more than

50 percent. These are significant numbers. The goal is to put together the entire matrix of the experience and maximize the overall experience rather than pieces within it. Opportunities to ensure optimal patient scheduling and eliminate time spent looking for pertinent information, and more, combine to improve the overall patient experience.

The hospital biggest challenge now is staffing all the proposed projects. "Opportunities are everywhere. Anyone can walk around and think how can they make this better for customers? Those customers include patients, staff, doctors, everybody. Everything can be addressed and improved.

Chapter 17: Ways Lean Healthcare Management Reduces Cost

With the financial pressures that healthcare organizations are facing, many hospitals are using traditional cost cutting methods to save money by looking at layoffs and staff reductions. Many more hospitals, however, are finding ways to reduce costs through lean management methods that don't require layoffs and can improve quality for patients.

Lean is actually the best alternative to layoffs. It's all about encouraging everyone to participate in process improvement, as well as finding creative and interesting ways to save money for a healthcare organization to avoid those unwanted traditional cost slashing endeavours like layoffs. Layoffs don't lead to long-term cost reduction. And if you lay off people and don't fix any processes, you are risking patient safety and quality. As a result, more and more healthcare providers are looking at lean to break that cycle.

Below are different ways that lean management can help reduce system cost.

1. Reduce never events. A "never event" includes falls, infections, erroneous amputations and other small-to-large-scale disasters. Reducing these events is, of course, best for patients, but there's also financial pressure to reduce never events. In 2009 in the US, Medicare stopped paying for care from events they consider preventable, and now private insurers are following suit. Pressure ulcers and bedsores, for example, are viewed as preventable. They should not happen if a good process is followed; like patients being repositioned. Improving quality in general saves hospitals more than layoffs since "never events" occur when an understaffed hospital can't be attentive enough to a patient needs.

2. Supply chain improvements. It is important to consider looking at a more effective material restocking process. For example, more frequent smaller batch deliveries or rotating supplies more quickly reduces both the amount of space used in internal warehouse and cash tied-up in inventory.

3. Delay or cancel construction and expansion. A trend in the last few years has shown that hospitals use lean to increase capacity by using current equipment and available space. Lean makes better use of existing resources as an alternative to increasing capital spending. "I worked with one hospital that through process improvement to patient flow; preventing delays from registration through to discharge they increased the utilization rates of their MRI machines from 40 percent to 60 percent. And they did not need to buy more equipment.

4. Reduce overtime. Reducing overtime is a great opportunity to help make improvements with lean that doesn't alienate people the way layoffs do. Essentially, people want to get home to have dinner with their families in a predictable/consistent way. If you can improve charting during the process, for example, instead of having nurses do it after, you can improve staff satisfaction while trimming down overtime, which results in both morale and cost savings. It is a win-win opportunity.

5. Reduce length of stay. This certainly isn't about pushing patients home before they are ready. Reducing length of stay is done through preventing errors that would extend a stay or delay a discharge when patients are medically ready to go home. Because of miscommunication, poor planning, or when families or nursing homes are not yet ready to take on the person being discharged, a four-day stay can suddenly turn into a five or six day stay. This process related things are not medical issues, but they often extend length of stay which can cost millions.

6. Reduce unnecessary testing and diagnostics. A number of hospitals are trying to be responsible stewards of healthcare pounds by reducing inappropriate usage of lab testing and diagnostic imaging. For example, through medical evidence it is been shown that when a patient comes in with back pain more often than not what they need is physical therapy not a fast pass to a CT scan.

7. Reduce delays and errors in billing. There are a tremendous amount of delays in billing, including too many people involved during different parts of the process. If there is a better flow, if people are handing off the work to the next person in the chain immediately, bills go out in a couple of days instead of a couple weeks. It is also incredibly important to make sure billing is being done properly. If mistakes are made and proper pre-authorizations are not followed, but procedures are done anyway, hospitals might be voluntarily giving away revenue.

Chapter 18: How Lean Help Drive Personalized Healthcare

There is growing interest in personalized medicine. Patients are increasingly being told that their care can be tailored to their specific situation. Enthusiasm for this approach is fuelled in part by advances in genetics (e.g. defining tumour-specific abnormalities in the genome) and therapeutics (e.g. targeted therapies that exploit unique biochemical/genetic abnormalities in tumours). Further, this approach "sounds good" and plays well to our sense of individualism and empowerment.

Concurrently, lean healthcare is being promoted as a means to improve clinical operations and efficiency through standardization and the reduction of waste. Lean approaches gained much credibility as they were successfully applied by Toyota to generate uniquely reliable automobiles. Similar lean-based improvements have been seen by other manufacturers as well as in other industries such as aviation.

Lean has been less vigorously embraced by healthcare. There are several well-known successes where lean has helped to improve operational efficiencies, increase financial performance and improve clinical outcomes. The standardization that comes with lean reduced inter-patient variations in care, appears to reduce errors, increases efficiency, and improves outcomes. In other words, exactly what was seen by Toyota. Nevertheless, it is very challenging to implement lean principles in healthcare. Indeed, the successes at some hospital took many years to be attained, and were hindered by much resistance from providers and staff alike.

Doctors and other care-providers are typically strong-willed and opinionated. The concept of standardization (fundamental to lean) is often seen by providers as an affront to their medical judgment, competence and professionalism. "We are not making cars, we are curing cancer" is a representative refrain voiced by opponents of lean.

Who is right? Like most things, the truth is somewhere in the middle. Healthcare providers indeed are not making cars, and inter-patient differences are almost certainly larger than the inter-car differences. Nevertheless, viewed from a fairly high level, patients and cars are very similar. In our local hospital radiation oncology clinic, they typically evaluate and care for over 100 patients per day, with a wide variety of ailments. There are many inter-patient differences that need to be considered on an individual basis, with corresponding modifications to their radiation doses, field sizes, etc.

Nevertheless, there are many commonalities that span across all patients. At the time of initial consultation, essentially all patients will have (in the same order) an evaluation by a nurse and doctor examination by a doctor, review of pertinent medical records, a recommendation for treatment (or not), and a series of appointments made for future activities. Sure there are differences in the details of these various components, but the broad structure can be readily standardized. Similarly, just prior to receiving a radiation treatment, essentially all patients will disrobe, get onto a table in the radiation treatment room, be positioned and aligned as needed, imaged to assume correct positioning, and then treated.

Therefore, lean concepts such as standardization can usually be readily applied to the broad aspects of patient care. However, as one delves more deeply into the details of any individual patient's treatments, the presence of (necessary) inter-patient variation makes the application of standardization more challenging.

The successful implementation of lean in healthcare requires that we accept that there are inter-patient differences and that the provider's input as to how to address these differences is still needed. Indeed, the goal of lean in healthcare is to standardize what can be standardized, so that the providers can spend their time focusing on those important inter-patient differences. In fact, it is those inter-patient differences that makes healthcare so interesting, challenging, and rewarding. Used properly, lean can liberate providers to relish the most interesting aspects of their work. Personalized medicine and lean healthcare are synergistic.

Chapter 19: How Lean Improve Healthcare Delivery

I am encouraged to see healthcare leaders looking beyond the ways they have always done things in the past to implementing innovative solutions such as Lean to curb the industry's skyrocketing costs, poor quality, nursing shortages and employee dissatisfaction; all symptoms of deeper problems inherent in the system itself.

Today's forward looking healthcare providers have realized the financial and moral imperatives for improving quality and safety and eliminating waste as strategies for responding to their pressing challenges.

Lean Healthcare (adapted from the Toyota Production System) is not just for manufacturing or another short-term fix; it's a way to transform an entire organization into a safe and high-quality, high-performing healthcare delivery system. If implemented properly, it can be the "how to" for managing change and creating continuous improvement.

Lean Healthcare is used to eliminate obstacles that prevent organizations from providing best-in-class healthcare by eliminating issues as vast as out-of-date technology systems, worker frustration and errors and oversights that can increase patient safety risks. Some "fixes" are complex, but lean methodology strives to find well-thought-out improvements that can be implemented quickly and without costing a fortune, if at all possible; thus the name Lean.

As a leader, it makes sense to at least research whether your organization would embrace the methodology and sustained results derived from lean implementation.

Below are ways hospital executives can improve cash flow through lean efforts.

1. Identify the Key Players in the Team

Before you implement any changes it is important to listen to what your people on the ground are saying. Before you embark on a lean journey coordinate a week when members from every step of the billing workflow, including nurses and hospital executives, met for five eight-hour days to brainstorm, goal set and devise a plan of attack. Sharing their interaction in the billing process will give needed insight to help find where waste occurs and where and how it can be feasibly prevented.

It is understandable that many healthcare executives may be afraid of taking employees off the ward for such a long period of time; however frontloading the planning accomplishes 40 to 50 hours of planning in one week that could otherwise take a year of hour-long weekly meetings. This not only keeps all parties on the same page when changes are launched, but it allows for better accountability and easier on-the-spot adjustments while plans are implemented.

2. Share Ideas and Prioritize Solutions

During the planning week, have attendees make diagrams of the billing workflow using Post-Its describing each step of the process and each department's role in advancing claims. This is called Value Stream Mapping and helps everybody identify where problems are occurring.

Once the process has been identified, attendees can brainstorm possible solutions and improvements to the current system, and then prioritized those solutions into four groups based on how cost and time effective each would be. This will help the team see multiple ways to confront the problem at the lowest cost and with the greatest chance of successful follow-through.

3. Implementation

Now you have a plan in place, it is vital to implement it effectively. This will take commitment from the whole planning team and involves a lot of checking to ensure processes are being followed correctly. Once the process is up and running it is also useful to make changes where necessary. Training is a big part of this, as well as streamlining processes.

4. Accountability

Ensure accountability for those responsible for implementing the changes. It is essential to realise the importance of accountability and to ensure there are checks in place to make sure the new processes are being adhered to.

Empowering staff members to identify and address waste at the ground level helps to maintain those efficiency improvements organically without the need to devote an entire week to planning sessions. The solution is to educate more people and get more looking for waste in their area.

Chapter 20: Conclusion

While Lean improvement methods have delivered higher efficiency and better quality products, the question of applicability in healthcare is still clouded by uncertainty. Traditionally, there have been opposing views; on the one hand promoting large-scale industrial-type improvement to bring healthcare into the modern era and, on the other, arguing that people are not motor cars and that simplistic adoption will only exacerbate the extreme difficulties of delivering uniform, high-quality, care within tight resources to populations whose expectations continue to rise.

As global healthcare expenditure soars above \$3.2 trillion, and as systems are increasingly required to deliver better care to more people using less resource, the challenge to explore the promises of Lean Thinking is compelling.

Lean Thinking is now widely recognized in care delivery circles around the world and there is a growing corpus of good news stories, guides and journal papers. As we show elsewhere, the adoption trend for Lean in healthcare appears to involve ad hoc practice, and so the fact that Lean approaches are widely articulated need not indicate that the process is particularly or exclusively Lean. Staff may, for instance, be describing an improvement initiative generally understood to be within the spirit of Lean. Having said that, there is evidence that improvement methods are bedding down in healthcare.

To bring some focus to what is a fast-moving and perhaps blurred scene; I identify three critical challenges that face Lean if it is to be more widely applied in a more discriminating fashion by delivery communities around the world.

1. Evidence

Adoption of new practices in healthcare is more related to evidence than is the case in managing a factory. In fact, there is an interesting cultural difference between the improvement communities and clinical communities. In medicine, the controlled trial, ideally a randomized control trial (RCT) is the gold standard but need not be large. For instance, one could argue that Christiaan Barnard's first heart transplant was a clinical trial with a sample size of one and showed that something as extraordinary as transplanting a human heart led to a better outcome than immediate death. In terms of improvement, controlled trials are possible, although there are clearly difficulties in terms of blinding participants and ensuring that trial behaviour and control behaviour stay within limits. A key factor here is the uncertainty inherent in healthcare, leading to a culture of evidence in which the effectiveness of a treatment for an individual patient is difficult to assess and, instead, groups are compared.

The world of improvement is quite different, driven by champions and fuelled with good news stories; the original "gurus" of quality management have been long on prescription but shorter on analysis, and moreover, have differed among themselves. This lack

106

of focus on the potential downside of interventions, plus a less complex analytical structure, makes it difficult to provide evidence of effectiveness to clinical communities.

These cultural differences champion versus researcher, good news versus analysis, trials versus improvement cycles run deep, and it will take a conceptual effort to provide systems of evidence gathering that will prove conclusive to each side.

2. Value

Although the concept of value is central to Lean, healthcare is a world full of values. We have proposed that there are at least three dimensions germane to healthcare; clinical, operational and experiential value. We further contend that most Lean in healthcare is essentially driven by an operational concept of value, and that the infrastructure does not yet exist adequately to trade, for instance, an extra day in hospital for a very slightly better outcome or, more difficult still, a better experience.

However achieved, Lean needs a common value currency so that improvement cycles can be driven to better outcomes as well as for better patient experience or efficiency gains.

3. Metrics

The key thing about metrics, especially when combined with a system of incentives, is that people try to achieve their metrics. For instance, the UK government expected General Practices to average around 75% in their Quality and Outcomes Framework metrics when the system was rolled out. The initial average of over 91% rose to nearly 97% in 3 years, creating a funding problem. This opens up a range of behaviours and games that people will play in order to meet their metrics.

In organizations where metrics already play a significant role there may be less incentive to start experimenting with local Lean improvements. However, where such metrics can be channelled into improvement cycles, one of the great strengths of Lean is that it encourages those working at the coal face, so to speak, to focus on increasing value and eliminating waste. Clearly, measurement is needed to show the local team that improvement is taking place (and therefore to guide the process) and also to justify to higher management and other stakeholders that the team is pulling its weight.

The key element, however, is the extent to which the Lean measures align with other key metrics within the institution human resources and finance, for instance or the wider values of the organization. Two major problems are the possibility of conflicting metrics on the one hand, where metrics' achieved in one field are at the expense of success in another, and of completely disconnected metrics, in which staff members face a mass of incomprehensible and unrelated targets.

Given consensus on evidence, value and metrics, there is no reason why Lean should not become a vital element in a world that is focused on process, governed by performance measures and, increasingly, guided by a core set of values.

Keep improving!!

Resource and References

Shigeo Shingo, Norman Bodek, Collin McLoughlin: Kaizen and the Art of Creative Thinking - The Scientific Thinking Mechanism

Shigeo Shingo; Fundamental Principles of Lean Manufacturing

Shigeo Shingo, Andrew P. Dillon (Translator); Zero Quality Control: Source Inspection and the Poka-yoke System

Shigeo Shingo; Non-Stock Production: The Shingo System of Continuous Improvement

Shigeo Shingo; A Study of the Toyota Production System from an Industrial Engineering Viewpoint

Shigeo Shingo; A Study of the Toyota Production System from an Industrial Engineering Viewpoint

Drucker, P. (1993) Post-Capitalist Society

Drucker, P., "What Makes an Effective Executive", Harvard Business review, June 2004

Lessons from Toyota's long drive, an interview with Katsuaki Watanabe, HBR, July 2007

Liker, J. & D. Meier, Toyota Talent, McGraw Hill, 2007

Shook, J. , Managing To Learn, Lean Enterprise Institute 2008

Fishman, C., "No Satisfaction", Fast Company, Dec 2006/Jan 2007

Womack, J. & J. Shook, Lean Management and The Role of Lean Leadership, Lean Enterprise Institute presentation, Oct. 2006